dare to Soar
A TEEN JOURNAL

paula white

PUBLISHED BY

BRONZE
BOW PUB.

All Scriptures are taken from the New King James Version. Copyright © 1982 by Thomas
Nelson, Inc. Used by permission. All rights reserved.

ISBN 1-932458-40-9

Published by Bronze Bow Publishing, Inc. and Paula White Ministries.

Bronze Bow Publishing Inc.,
2600 E. 26th Street, Minneapolis, MN 55406
You can reach Bronze Bow Publishing on the Internet
at www.bronzebowpublishing.com.

Paula White Ministries
P.O. Box 25151
Tampa, Florida 33622
You can reach Paula White Ministries on the Internet
at www.paulawhite.org.

Literary development and cover/interior design by Koechel Peterson & Associates, Inc.,
Minneapolis, Minnesota.

Manufactured in Hong Kong

I can do all things

through Christ

who strengthens me.

PHILIPPIANS 4:13

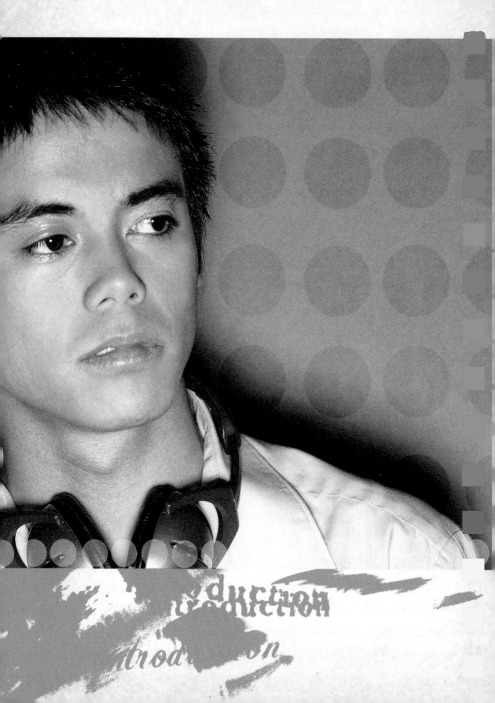

Did you know that you are the apple of God's eye?

Did you know that God looks forward to spending time with you every day? You are so special to God. He hung the stars and the moon just for you. He chose the color of your eyes, your height, and even your quirky sense of humor. He made you so uniquely special that nobody in the entire world is just like you. There has never been and will never be another you! How cool is that?

God never makes mistakes.

He created you for a unique and special purpose. You are in this world for a reason . . . a BIG reason! There is something huge for you to accomplish through your life, and you can start making steps to achieve it today! Sometimes we are afraid to follow our hopes and dreams because we don't really believe that we can accomplish them. Through God, nothing is impossible! That means anything you can dream of, you can achieve!

You were created by God,

destined for great things. All you have to do is believe in yourself, and believe what God says about you. What does God say? He says that you were fearfully and wonderfully made. That means that He took time and formed every part of you to be in His image, yet totally YOU! He deposited in you everything you will ever need to accomplish the dreams and goals that He has for you.

How do you unlock the hidden treasures

that God has placed within you? How do you find out what God would have you to do? Spend time with God. Talk to Him! Through prayer, you have full access to God! You can talk to Him about anything, and He will answer you! Use this journal as a way to communicate with God. Write down questions that you are seeking answers to, and anything that you would like to share with Him. He is a Friend, a Brother, and a Father. God is everything you need Him to be.

What would God have you do

today to prepare for your dreams and goals? What can you do to become more of the person whom God has created you to be? What obstacles are you facing in your relationship with God? Your daily thoughts will tell the story.

WHY JOURNAL?

As you grow and mature into the person God has created you to be, your personal experience with God should be kept in a journal to always remind you of your thoughts, your prayers, and your growth. I want you to freely express your thoughts on any area of your life that God shines His light upon—whether it is your personality, your prayer life, your relationship with friends, your career interests, your looks, a dating relationship, your hobbies, your faith, your parents or a sibling, the good stuff and the bad stuff, or whatever. Express what you are discovering about yourself. Say whatever is on your heart. And focus on how God is teaching you to fly, the lessons and truths He is working in your life. Whenever God speaks, His message is always worth recording, and it will always strengthen your wings for flight.

Journaling is an exercise that has enhanced my faith walk and has revealed God's faithfulness in my life as I have learned to trust Him. It has created a lasting record of my conversations with God. In journal time, God's voice is loudest in my life. It's through my volumes and volumes of journals that I have found a lasting record of my friendship with God.

I wish the very same for you.

Paula

I've always kept a journal, and I have cherished the privilege of speaking directly to God through prayer since the day I put my faith in Jesus Christ. So prayer journaling, in particular, came quite naturally to me. What I didn't know early on was that I would actually be able to have conversations with God, to talk to and hear back from Him. The big fancy words of the King James Bible intimidated me. I thought I had to speak to God in the language of Abraham or David. Not so.

When you speak to God, it does not have to be formal. James 2:23 says that because Abraham believed in God, he was a friend of God. Do you believe in God? Well, then you, too, are His friend. Formal words such as *thee* and *thou* can be put aside for casual terms such as *Daddy* and *Father*. He just wants to hear from you. Speak to Him from your heart, and He will speak to you from His.

Dedicating a "journal time" each day will help you to get into the routine of journaling. Choose a quiet, private place to shut out the cares of the world and steal away with God. Perhaps a good time for you is just before bed or in the morning before the rest of your family awakes. It may help to play soothing worship music to calm your mind.

Be sure to list the date at the beginning of each entry. This will be particularly interesting to you as you reflect back over the pages later on. Then check the box that best describes your journal entry for the day. Are you expressing discoveries you are making about yourself? Are you recording how God is strengthening your wings and teaching you to fly? Take as much space as you need to jot down whatever you feel or are thinking, running into several pages if necessary. Allow yourself to flow freely, releasing any tensions, anxieties, or worries to God through your pen. Talk to Him, listen to Him, commune with Him. The more often you do it, the more natural it will feel.

Habakkuk 2:2 encourages us to "write the vision and make it plain on tablets, that he may run who reads it." Periodically throughout this journal, you will find "Reflections" pages. These pages are intended to give you an opportunity to review several entries at a time so that you can see your own personal growth and to remind you of the desires you have written. They also provide you the opportunity to reflect on all that God has spoken to you and performed in your life. Take every opportunity to appreciate the smallest answered prayer and to meditate on God's faithfulness.

Dear God,
Show Yourself to me today.
Give me wisdom to make decisions
as You teach me,
by making Your way known.
Teach me how
to be more like You.

[ ] Today's thoughts...

[ ] How I'm learning to soar...

For I know the thoughts that I think toward you, says the LORD, thoughts of peace and not of evil, to give you a future and a hope. Then you will call upon Me and go and pray to Me, and I will listen to you. And you will seek Me and find Me, when you search for Me with all your heart.

JEREMIAH 29:11–13

Quit comparing yourself to everyone around you and
copying what they're doing. You are the designer's original.

[ ] Today's thoughts...

       [ ] How I'm learning to soar...

What you believe about yourself virtually dictates how successful you are in every area of your life.

DATE
....

[ ] today's thoughts...

    [ ] how i'm learning to soar...

for You formed my
inward parts; You
covered me in my
mother's womb. I
will praise You, for
I am fearfully and
wonderfully made;
marvelous are Your
works, and that
my soul knows
very well.

PSALM 139:13-14

marvelous are Y...
marvelous are Your...

DATE

[ ] today's thoughts...

[ ] how i'm learning to soar...

DATE

[ ] Today's thoughts...

[ ] How I'm learning to soar...

Your hands have made me and fashioned me; give me

understanding, that I may learn Your commandments.

PSALM 119:73

[ ] Today's thoughts...

[ ] How I'm learning to soar...

God made you precisely and perfectly. You are the "right" gender, race, personality, body shape, and height. He knew what He was doing.

[ ] Today's thoughts...

[ ] How I'm learning to soar...

"Bring My sons
from afar, and
My daughters
from the ends
of the earth—
everyone who is
called by My
name, whom I
have created
for My glory; I
have formed
him, yes, I
have made him."

ISAIAH 43:6-7

[ ] Today's thoughts...

[ ] How I'm learning to soar...

[ ] Today's thoughts...

    [ ] How I'm learning to soar...

You are filled with endless potential and possibilities.

[ ] **Today's thoughts...**

[ ] **How I'm learning to soar...**

But to each one

of us grace was

given according

to the measure of

Christ's gift.

EPHESIANS 4:7

potential and possibilities

DATE

[ ] Today's thoughts...

[ ] How I'm learning to soar...

As a man thinketh

in his heart,

so is he.

PROVERBS 4:23 KJV

[ ] Today's thoughts...

[ ] How I'm learning to soar...

It's not what we see in
the mirror that defines
who we are.

[ ] Today's thoughts...

      [ ] How I'm learning to soar...

Don't let life falsely label you. God will make you
"larger than life."

"For the LORD does not see as man sees; for man looks at the outward appearance, but the LORD looks at the heart."

1 SAMUEL 16:7

[ ] Today's thoughts . . .

[ ] How I'm Learning to soar . . .

[ ] today's thoughts...

[ ] how i'm learning to soar...

Jesus answered and
said to her,
"Whoever drinks of
this water will
thirst again, but
whoever drinks of
the water that I
shall give him will
never thirst. But
the water that I
shall give him will
become in him a
fountain of water
springing up into
everlasting life."

JOHN 4:13-14

[ ] today's thoughts...

[ ] how i'm learning to soar...

You must daily derive your life from Jesus—
your fountain of living water.

"For God so loved the world that He gave His only begotten Son, that whoever believes in Him should not perish but have everlasting life."

JOHN 3:16

[ ] Today's thoughts...

[ ] How I'm learning to soar...

[ ] Today's thoughts...

[ ] How I'm learning to soar...

GOD LOVED THE BROKEN YOU.

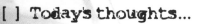

....

[ ] Today's thoughts...

[ ] How I'm learning to soar...

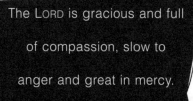

The LORD is gracious and full

of compassion, slow to

anger and great in mercy.

PSALM 145:8

[ ] Today's thoughts...

[ ] How I'm learning to soar...

You cannot love others until you love yourself. You cannot truly love yourself until you know and experience God's love for you.

DATE

[ ] Today's thoughts...

[ ] How I'm learning to soar...

> Every word of God is pure; He is a shield to those who put their trust in Him.
>
> PROVERBS 30:5

stop living by what you feel and live by what God says.

[ ] *Today's thoughts...*

[ ] *How I'm learning to soar...*

[ ] Today's thoughts . . .

[ ] How I'm learning to soar . . .

> For it is God who
> works in you both to
> will and to do for
> His good pleasure.
>
> PHILIPPIANS 2:13

[ ] **Today's thoughts . . .**

[ ] **How I'm learning to soar . . .**

You have been
engineered by God
to be a success.

[ ] *Today's thoughts...*

    [ ] *How I'm learning to soar...*

"I have come that
they may have
life, and that
they may have it
more abundantly."

JOHN 10:10

[ ] *Today's thoughts...*

[ ] *How I'm learning to soar...*

You must "think big"
to do God-sized
things.

DATE

....

[ ] Today's thoughts...

           [ ] How I'm learning to soar...

"But you shall receive

power when the Holy

Spirit has come upon

you; and you shall be

witnesses to Me in

Jerusalem, and in all

Judea and Samaria, and

to the end of the earth."

ACTS 1:8

The real p

exp

[ ] Today's thoughts...

[ ] How I'm learning to soar...

The real power of God is released when you experience it in a personal way.

....

[ ] Today's thoughts...

        [ ] How I'm learning to soar...

Finally, my brethren,

be strong in the Lord

and in the power of

His might.

EPHESIANS 6:10

[ ] Today's thoughts...

[ ] How I'm learning to soar...

God has placed His strength where your
weakness was.

"And you shall know the truth, and the truth shall make you free."

J O H N 8 : 3 2

[ ] Today's thoughts . . .

[ ] How I'm learning to soar . . .

[ ] Today's thoughts...

[ ] How I'm learning to soar...

God Loves you too
much to leave you
the same.

[ ] Today's thoughts...

[ ] How I'm learning to soar...

Now to Him who is able to do
exceedingly abundantly above all
that we ask or think, according to
the power that works in us, to Him
be glory in the church by Christ
Jesus to all generations, forever
and ever. Amen.

EPHESIANS 3:20–21

[ ] Today's thoughts...

[ ] How I'm learning to soar...

> There is power
> working inwardly
> that is much
> greater
> than anything
> exteriorly.

DATE

[ ] Today's thoughts...

[ ] How I'm learning to soar...

Your word I have

hidden in my heart,

that I might not sin

against You.

PSALM 119:11

[ ] Today's thoughts...

[ ] How I'm learning to soar...

God transforms me
with His truths.

[ ] Today's thoughts . . .

[ ] How I'm learning to soar . . .

Remove falsehood

and lies far

from me.

PROVERBS 30:8

[ ] Today's thoughts . . .

[ ] How I'm learning to soar . . .

Right is right if no one is doing it, and wrong
is wrong if everyone is doing it.

[ ] Today's thoughts...

[ ] How I'm learning to soar...

Do not fret because of evildoers, nor be envious of the workers of iniquity. For they shall soon be cut down like the grass, and wither as the green herb. Trust in the LORD, and do good; dwell in the land, and feed on His faithfulness. Delight yourself also in the LORD, and He shall give you the desires of your heart.

PSALM 37:1–4

[ ] *Today's thoughts...*

[ ] *How I'm learning to soar...*

You don't
have to be
sinful to
still be
exciting!

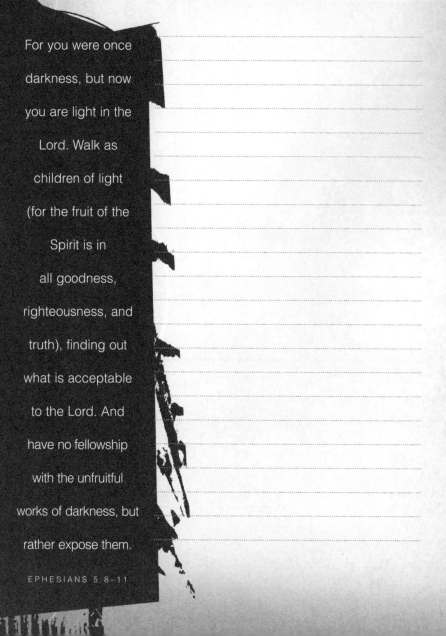

DATE
···

[ ] Today's thoughts...

[ ] How I'm learning to soar...

For you were once darkness, but now you are light in the Lord. Walk as children of light (for the fruit of the Spirit is in all goodness, righteousness, and truth), finding out what is acceptable to the Lord. And have no fellowship with the unfruitful works of darkness, but rather expose them.

EPHESIANS 5:8–11

[ ] Today's thoughts...

[ ] How I'm learning to soar...

As long as you say, "Someday ... I'm going to get out," you postpone your deliverance! You must transition your thinking to ... Today!

You were created by God to not just fly as a common bird but to soar as the eagle does. God gave you gifts and hopes and desires and a personality that is uniquely yours. But you have to dare to spread your wings, turn and face the wind, and trust the air to lift you high—you have to have faith that God will hold you up. How high will you soar?

Take time to review the last several pages of this journal. Reflect on all the things you have been discovering about your life. As you've thought about your life in the light of God's Word, what are you learning? How is God teaching you to fly? What lessons and truths is He working in your life?

Capture your thoughts below.

[ ] today's thoughts...

[ ] how i'm learning to soar...

"Choose for yourselves this

day whom you will serve,

whether the gods which your

fathers served that were on

the other side of the River, or

the gods of the Amorites, in

whose land you dwell. But as

for me and my house, we will

serve the LORD."

JOSHUA 24:15

[ ] Today's thoughts...

      [ ] How I'm learning to soar...

challenge yourself out of your comfort zone and
into your commitment zone.

"*Assuredly, I say to you, all sins will be forgiven the sons of men, and whatever blasphemies they may utter.*"

MARK 3:28

[ ] Today's thoughts...

[ ] How I'm learning to soar...

[ ] Today's thoughts . . .

[ ] How I'm learning to soar . . .

God will always give you another chance:
the choice is yours to take it.

[ ] Today's thoughts...

[ ] How I'm learning to soar...

"Come now, and let

us reason together,"

says the LORD,

"though your sins are

like scarlet, they shall

be as white as snow;

though they are red

like crimson, they

shall be as wool. If

you are willing and

obedient, you shall

eat the good of

the land."

ISAIAH 1:18-19

[ ] Today's thoughts...

[ ] How I'm learning to soar...

GOD WANTS TO
DEAL WITH THE
"REAL YOU!"

DATE

[ ] Today's thoughts...

 [ ] How I'm learning to soar...

Do not be

deceived: "Evil

company corrupts

good habits."

1 CORINTHIANS 15:33

[ ] Today's thoughts...

[ ] How I'm learning to soar...

People either add, subtract, multiply,
or divide in your life.

DATE

[ ] today's thoughts...

[ ] how i'm learning to soar...

He who walks with

wise men will be

wise, but the com-

panion of fools will

be destroyed.

PROVERBS 13:20

[ ] today's thoughts...

[ ] how i'm learning to soar...

Who your friends
are determines
who you are.

....

[ ] Today's thoughts . . .

        [ ] How I'm learning to soar . . .

The righteous

should choose his

friends carefully, for

the way of the

wicked leads them

astray.

PROVERBS 12:26

[ ] Today's thoughts...

[ ] How I'm learning to soar...

No one becomes
successful by
accident.

DATE

....

[ ] *Today's thoughts...*

    [ ] *How I'm learning to soar...*

For we have spent enough of our past lifetime in doing the
will of the Gentiles—when we walked in lewdness, lusts,
drunkenness, revelries, drinking parties, and abominable
idolatries. In regard to these, they think it strange that you
do not run with them in the same flood of dissipation,
speaking evil of you.

1 PETER 4:3–4

[ ] Today's thoughts . . .

        [ ] How I'm learning to soar . . .

(*)

often "old friends"
don't understand
the "new change"
in you.

[ ] *Today's thoughts...*

    [ ] *How I'm learning to soar...*

A friend loves at all

times, and a brother

is born for adversity.

PROVERBS 17:17

[ ] *Today's thoughts...*

[ ] *How I'm learning to soar...*

A TRUE FRIEND SEES BEYOND WHAT YOU ARE
TO WHAT YOU CAN BE.

DATE

....

[ ] Today's thoughts...

        [ ] How I'm learning to soar...

What enters your life determines what will exit.

[ ] Today's thoughts . . .

[ ] How I'm learning to soar . . .

Keep your heart

with all diligence,

for out of it spring

the issues of life.

PROVERBS 4:23

[ ] **Today's thoughts...**

　　　　　　[ ] **How I'm learning to soar...**

Turn away my eyes

from looking at

worthless things,

and revive me in

Your way.

PSALM 119:37

[ ] Today's thoughts...

[ ] How I'm learning to soar...

Admit it and
quit it.

[ ] Today's thoughts...

   [ ] How I'm learning to soar...

Perfect faith cannot exist where the
will of God is unknown.

[ ] **Today's thoughts...**

[ ] **How I'm learning to soar...**

> And do not be
> conformed to this
> world, but be
> transformed by the
> renewing of your
> mind, that you may
> prove what is
> that good and
> acceptable and
> perfect will of God.
>
> ROMANS 12:2

where the
own.

[ ] today's thoughts...

  [ ] how i'm learning to soar...

But one thing I do, forgetting those things which are behind

and reaching forward to those things which are ahead, I

press toward the goal for the prize of the upward call of

God in Christ Jesus.

PHILIPPIANS 3:13-14

[ ] Today's thoughts...

[ ] How I'm learning to soar...

Opening the door to your future requires shutting
the door to your past.

[ ] Today's thoughts . . .

[ ] How I'm learning to soar . . .

If any of you lacks wisdom, let him ask of God, who gives to all liberally and without reproach, and it will be given to him. But let him ask in faith, with no doubting, for he who doubts is like a wave of the sea driven and tossed by the wind. For let not that man suppose that he will receive anything from the Lord; he is a double-minded man, unstable in all his ways.

[ ] *Today's thoughts...*

[ ] *How I'm learning to soar...*

You cannot look ahead and look behind you
at the same time.

[ ] Today's thoughts . . .

[ ] How I'm learning to soar . . .

"Therefore keep the
words of this
covenant, and do
them, that you may
prosper in all that
you do."

DEUTERONOMY 29:9

[ ] Today's thoughts . . .

[ ] How I'm learning to soar . . .

Don't let your history hinder you
from your destiny.

DATE

[ ] Today's thoughts...

      [ ] How I'm learning to soar...

Everything you
need in life is
within you.
Discover your
resources and
develop them.

[ ] Today's thoughts . . .

[ ] How I'm learning to soar . . .

Let not mercy and

truth forsake you;

bind them around

your neck, write

them on the tablet

of your heart.

PROVERBS 3:3

DATE
....

[ ] *Today's thoughts...*

[ ] *How I'm learning to soar...*

When you know
who you are, you
don't have to
struggle to live
up to what
someone has
defined you
to be.

[ ] *Today's thoughts...*

[ ] *How I'm learning to soar...*

In God (I will praise His word), in the LORD (I will praise His word), in God I have put my trust; I will not be afraid. What can man do to me?

PSALM 56:10–11

[ ] Today's thoughts...

[ ] How I'm learning to soar...

Now may the God of peace who brought up our Lord Jesus
from the dead, that great Shepherd of the sheep, through
the blood of the everlasting covenant, make you complete
in every good work to do His will, working in you what is
well pleasing in His sight, through Jesus Christ, to whom
be glory forever and ever. Amen.

HEBREWS 13:20-21

[ ] Today's thoughts...

[ ] How I'm learning to soar...

When God calls
you, He equips
you.

[ ] Today's thoughts...

[ ] How I'm learning to soar...

By the grace of

God I am what I

am, and His grace

toward me was not

in vain.

1 CORINTHIANS 15:10

[ ] Today's thoughts...

[ ] How I'm learning to soar...

Don't spend a lifetime trying to be what you were
not created to be.

[ ] Today's thoughts...

[ ] How I'm learning to soar...

Having then gifts differing according to the grace that is given to us, let us use them: if prophecy, let us prophesy in proportion to our faith; or ministry, let us use it in our ministering; he who teaches, in teaching; he who exhorts, in exhortation; he who gives, with liberality; he who leads, with diligence; he who shows mercy, with cheerfulness.

ROMANS 12:6-8

It's time to discover new strength with

[ ] Today's thoughts...

[ ] How I'm learning to soar...

It's time
to discover
new strengths
within yourself
and build on
them to
achieve your
God-given
potential and
goals.

[ ] Today's thoughts . . .

        [ ] How I'm learning to soar . . .

The steps of a good

man are ordered by

the LORD, and He

delights in his way.

PSALM 37:23

[ ] Today's thoughts...

[ ] How I'm learning to soar...

There is a deposit of wealth within you waiting to be developed.

[ ] *Today's thoughts...*

[ ] *How I'm learning to soar...*

"Eye has not seen,

nor ear heard, nor

have entered into the

heart of man the

things which God has

prepared for those

who love Him." But

God has revealed

them to us through

His Spirit. For the

Spirit searches all

things, yes, the deep

things of God.

1 CORINTHIANS 2:9–10

ATE

[ ] *Today's thoughts...*

[ ] *How I'm learning to soar...*

Build a dream
beyond your
means.

As a young man, David took the skills and the faith he had
developed as a shepherd boy and soared to defeat the Philistine
champion Goliath. David had already killed a lion and a bear in
the defense of his lambs, and a giant who defied God was
merely a another brutal thug who would give way to one who
dared to rise above his fears and put his trust in the name of
the Lord. God had already strengthened David's wings to fly
(1 Samuel 17).

Take time to review the last several pages of this journal. Reflect
on all the things you have been discovering about your life. As
you've thought about your life in the light of God's Word, what
are you learning? How is God teaching you to fly? What lessons
and truths is He working in your life?

Capture your thoughts below.

[ ] Today's thoughts...

[ ] How I'm learning to soar...

Therefore, whether you eat or drink, or whatever you do,

do all to the glory of God.

1 CORINTHIANS 10:31

[ ] Today's thoughts...

[ ] How I'm learning to soar...

We were born
to make manifest
the glory of
God that is
within us.

[ ] **Today's thoughts . . .**

[ ] **How I'm learning to soar . . .**

What then shall we

say to these things?

If God is for us,

who can be against

us? He who did not

spare His own Son,

but delivered Him

up for us all, how

shall He not with

Him also freely give

us all things?

ROMANS 8:31-32

[ ] Today's thoughts...

[ ] How I'm learning to soar...

God is not intimidated by your aspirations.
He gave them to you, so go for it.

DATE

[ ] Today's thoughts . . .

[ ] How I'm learning to soar . . .

Jesus said to her,
"Did I not say to
you that if you
would believe you
would see the glory
of God?"

JOHN 11:40

[ ] Today's thoughts...

[ ] How I'm learning to soar...

Nothing big ever
comes from
thinking small.

[ ] today's thoughts...

[ ] how i'm learning to soar...

"For I will pour water on him who is

thirsty, and floods on the dry ground; I

will pour My Spirit on your descendants,

and My blessing on your offspring."

ISAIAH 44:3

[ ] today's thoughts...

[ ] how i'm learning to soar...

> You might be
> disappointed
> if you fail,
> but you are
> doomed if you
> never try.

DATE

....

[ ] today's thoughts...

[ ] how i'm learning to soar...

"You whom I have taken from the ends of the earth, and called from its farthest regions, and said to you, 'You are My servant, I have chosen you and have not cast you away: fear not, for I am with you; be not dismayed, for I am your God. I will strengthen you, yes, I will help you, I will uphold you with My righteous right hand.'"

[ ] Today's thoughts...

[ ] How I'm learning to soar...

Do not fear mistakes—fail your way to success.

....

[ ] *Today's thoughts...*

[ ] *How I'm learning to soar...*

My brethren, count

it all joy when you

fall into various

trials, knowing that

the testing of your

faith produces

patience. But let

patience have its

perfect work, that

you may be perfect

and complete,

lacking nothing.

JAMES 1:2-4

....

[ ] *Today's thoughts...*

[ ] *How I'm learning to soar...*

Trouble is an
incubator for
greatness.

DATE

[ ] Today's thoughts . . .

　　　　　[ ] How I'm learning to soar . . .

The Lᴏʀᴅ my God will enlighten my
darkness. For by You I can run
against a troop, by my God I can
leap over a wall. As for God, His
way is perfect; the word of the
Lᴏʀᴅ is proven; He is a shield to all
who trust in Him.

PSALM 18:28-30

[ ] Today's thoughts . . .

[ ] How I'm learning to soar . . .

The door of
opportunity
swings on the
hinges of
opposition.

DATE

[ ] Today's thoughts...

        [ ] How I'm learning to soar...

For every blessing there is testing.
For every opportunity there is adversity.

[ ] Today's thoughts...

[ ] How I'm learning to soar...

"But He knows the

way that I take;

when He has tested

me, I shall come

forth as gold."

JOB 23:10

[ ] Today's thoughts . . .

[ ] How I'm learning to soar . . .

"Hear, O Israel:

Today you are on

the verge of battle

with your enemies.

Do not let your

heart faint, do not

be afraid, and do

not tremble or be

terrified because of

them; for the LORD

your God is He who

goes with you, to

fight for you against

your enemies, to

save you."

DEUTERONOMY 20:3–4

You g

[ ] Today's thoughts . . .

[ ] How I'm learning to soar . . .

You don't conquer without conflict.
You don't win without war.

[ ] Today's thoughts...

[ ] How I'm learning to soar...

As long as you don't quit, you will never lose.

[ ] Today's thoughts . . .

[ ] How I'm learning to soar . . .

"But those who wait

on the LORD shall

renew their

strength; they shall

mount up with

wings like eagles,

they shall run and

not be weary,

they shall walk

and not faint."

ISAIAH 40:31

"And from the days of John the Baptist until now the kingdom of heaven suffers violence, and the violent take it by force."

MATTHEW 11:12

[ ] Today's thoughts...

[ ] How I'm learning to soar...

[ ] Today's thoughts...

[ ] How I'm learning to soar...

PASSIONATE PEOPLE FIND THE POWER TO
PUSH THROUGH EVERY OBSTACLE HOLDING
THEM BACK!

[ ] Today's thoughts...

[ ] How I'm Learning to soar...

Praying always with

all prayer and

supplication in the

Spirit, being watchful

to this end with all

perseverance and

supplication for all

the saints.

EPHESIANS 6:18

[ ] Today's thoughts...

[ ] How I'm learning to soar...

If the enemy
can't get you
to quit, he
will get you
distracted.

[ ] Today's thoughts...

[ ] How I'm learning to soar...

For God has not

given us a spirit of

fear, but of power

and of love and of a

sound mind.

2 TIMOTHY 1:7

[ ] Today's thoughts...

[ ] How I'm learning to soar...

Recognize that those who reject you have no ability to see inside you.

[ ] Today's thoughts . . .

[ ] How I'm learning to soar . . .

"Many a time they have afflicted me from my youth; yet they have not prevailed against me. The plowers plowed on my back; they made their furrows long." The LORD is righteous; He has cut in pieces the cords of the wicked.

PSALM 129:2-4

[ ] Today's thoughts . . .

[ ] How I'm learning to soar . . .

You can handle rejection if you don't need
acceptance from the person rejecting you.

[ ] Today's thoughts . . .

[ ] How I'm learning to soar . . .

Then the LORD turned to him and said, "Go in this might of yours, and you shall save Israel from the hand of the Midianites. Have I not sent you?" So he said to Him, "O my Lord, how can I save Israel? Indeed my clan is the weakest in Manasseh, and I am the least in my father's house." And the LORD said to him, "Surely I will be with you, and you shall defeat the Midianites as one man."

JUDGES 6:14–16

[ ] Today's thoughts...

      [ ] How I'm learning to soar...

Little people
can do big
things.

DATE
....

[ ] today's thoughts...

[ ] how i'm learning to soar...

"For with God

nothing will be

impossible."

LUKE 1:37

[ ] todays thoughts...

[ ] how im learning to soar...

It is
scientifically
proven that the
bumblebee cannot
fly—his
wingspan is too
short for his
body weight—
but nobody
ever told
the bumblebee.

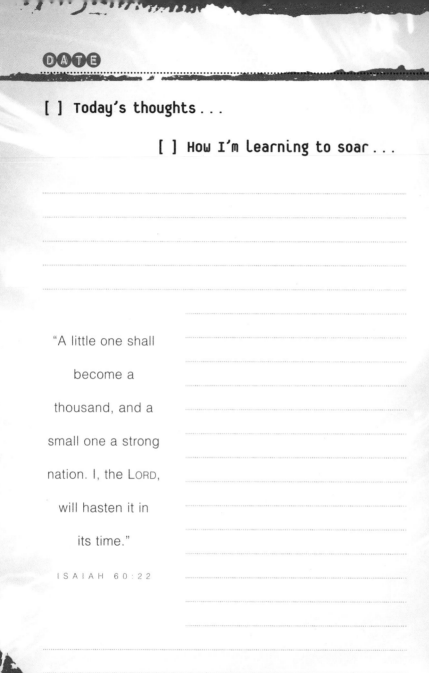

D A T E

[ ] Today's thoughts...

[ ] How I'm learning to soar...

"A little one shall

become a

thousand, and a

small one a strong

nation. I, the LORD,

will hasten it in

its time."

ISAIAH 60:22

[ ] Today's thoughts...

[ ] How I'm learning to soar...

Don't despise
small begin-
nings—they can
turn into large
endings.

....

[ ] *Today's thoughts...*

[ ] *How I'm learning to soar...*

"And it shall come
to pass afterward
that I will pour out
My Spirit on all
flesh; your sons and
your daughters
shall prophesy, your
old men shall
dream dreams, your
young men shall
see visions."

JOEL 2:28

[ ] *Today's thoughts...*

[ ] *How I'm learning to soar...*

God calls ordinary people to do extraordinary things.

[ ] Today's thoughts...

[ ] How I'm learning to soar...

But now, thus says the LORD, who created you, O Jacob,
and He who formed you, O Israel: "Fear not, for I have
redeemed you; I have called you by your name; you are
Mine. When you pass through the waters, I will be with you;
and through the rivers, they shall not overflow you. When
you walk through the fire, you shall not be burned, nor shall
the flame scorch you."

ISAIAH 43:1-2

[ ] Today's thoughts...

[ ] How I'm learning to soar...

A person with
a past can touch
a God in the
present who is
able to change
the future.

Then David said to [Goliath], "You come to me with a sword, with a spear, and with a javelin. But I come to you in the name of the LORD of hosts, the God of the armies of Israel, whom you have defied. This day the LORD will deliver you into my hand, and I will strike you and take your head from you."

1 SAMUEL 17:45–46

[ ] Today's thoughts . . .

[ ] How I'm learning to soar . . .

[ ] Today's thoughts . . .

[ ] How I'm learning to soar . . .

motivation is deeper than
words. motives have a lot to do
with who you are.

[ ] today's thoughts...

[ ] how i'm learning to soar...

Oh, that men would give thanks to the LORD for His goodness, and for His wonderful works to the children of men! For He satisfies the longing soul, and fills the hungry soul with goodness."

PSALM 107:8-9

[ ] today's thoughts...

[ ] how i'm learning to soar...

only hungry
minds can grow.

REFLECTIONS 3

If you've read the Book of Esther, you know that Esther was a young woman whose marvelous courage and wise actions were instrumental in the saving of her people. She held the key to the future of a nation, and her faith rose to the challenge: "I will go to the king, which is against the law; and if I perish, I perish!" (Esther 4:16). Her beliefs fueled her passion, and she soared upward to become an unstoppable force for good.

Take time to review the last several pages of this journal. Reflect on all the things you have been discovering about your life. As you've thought about your life in the light of God's Word, what are you learning? How is God teaching you to fly? What lessons and truths is He working in your life?

Capture your thoughts below.

[ ] Today's thoughts . . .

[ ] How I'm learning to soar . . .

Until you accept that God created you perfectly as you are,
you will try to be someone else, and that would be an imitation.

[ ] *Today's thoughts...*

[ ] *How I'm learning to soar...*

Where can I go from Your Spirit? Or where can I flee from Your presence? If I ascend into heaven, You are there; if I make my bed in hell, behold, You are there. If I take the wings of the morning, and dwell in the uttermost parts of the sea, even there Your hand shall lead me, and Your right hand shall hold me.

PSALM 139:7-10

[ ] *Today's thoughts...*

[ ] *How I'm learning to soar...*

Only those who risk going too far will ever know
how far they can go.

[ ] Today's thoughts...

      [ ] How I'm learning to soar...

"Therefore I say to

you, whatever

things you ask

when you pray,

believe that you

receive them, and

you will have them."

MARK 11:24

[ ] Today's thoughts . . .

[ ] How I'm learning to soar . . .

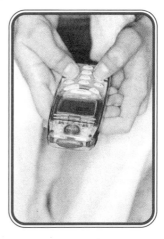

Begin to exhale
what God has
inhaled in you.

DATE

[ ] *Today's thoughts...*

    [ ] *How I'm learning to soar...*

"Therefore whoever hears these sayings of Mine, and does
them, I will liken him to a wise man who built his house on
the rock."

MATTHEW 7:24

[ ] *Today's thoughts...*

[ ] *How I'm learning to soar...*

Your future is determined by the decisions you
make, the priorities you develop, and the per-
spective you see things through.

DATE

[ ] Today's thoughts . . .

[ ] How I'm learning to soar . . .

Death and life are

in the power of the

tongue, and those

who love it will eat

its fruit.

PROVERBS 18:21

[ ] Today's thoughts...

[ ] How I'm learning to soar...

You frame your
world by the
words you speak.

DATE

[ ] Today's thoughts...

[ ] How I'm learning to soar...

And we know that

all things work

together for good to

those who love

God, to those who

are the called

according to His

purpose.

ROMANS 8:28

[ ] Today's thoughts...

[ ] How I'm learning to soar...

Your attitude determines your altitude.

[ ] Today's thoughts . . .

[ ] How I'm learning to soar . . .

For every person
there will be a
problem, but for
every problem
God has a
prescription.

[ ] Today's thoughts...

[ ] How I'm learning to soar...

And He said to me, "My grace is sufficient for you, for My

strength is made perfect in weakness."

2 CORINTHIANS 12:9

[ ] today's thoughts...

[ ] how i'm learning to soar...

Walk in the Spirit,

and you shall not

fulfill the lust of

the flesh.

GALATIANS 5:16

[ ] today's thoughts...

[ ] how i'm learning to soar...

Don't pursue what the Holy Ghost has already
rejected in your life.

DATE

[ ] Today's thoughts . . .

[ ] How I'm learning to soar . . .

Though [Jesus] was

a Son, yet He

learned obedience

by the things which

He suffered.

HEBREWS 5:8

[ ] Today's thoughts...

[ ] How I'm learning to soar...

To be
disciplined
means to do the
right thing when
you feel like
doing the
wrong thing.

DATE

....

[ ] Today's thoughts...

[ ] How I'm learning to soar...

But we all, with unveiled face, beholding as in a mirror the

glory of the Lord, are being transformed into the same

image from glory to glory, just as by the Spirit of the Lord.

2 CORINTHIANS 3:18

[ ] Today's thoughts...

[ ] How I'm learning to soar...

Defining moments are how you got to be the
person that you are.

DATE

"For where your treasure is, there your heart will be also."

MATTHEW 6:21

[ ] Today's thoughts...

[ ] How I'm learning to soar...

[ ] Today's thoughts...

[ ] How I'm learning to soar...

Where you spend
your money tells
you what you
value.

[ ] Today's thoughts . . .

[ ] How I'm learning to soar . . .

Let this mind be in
you which was also
in Christ Jesus,
who, being in the
form of God,
did not consider it
robbery to be equal
with God, but made
Himself of no
reputation, taking
the form of a
bondservant, and
coming in the
likeness of men.

PHILIPPIANS 2:5–7

[ ] Today's thoughts . . .

[ ] How I'm learning to soar . . .

Be flexible. You
will need to
bend in life.

DATE

....

[ ] today's thoughts...

[ ] how i'm learning to soar...

Rejoice in the Lord

always. Again I will

say, rejoice!

PHILIPPIANS 4:4

[ ] today's thoughts...

[ ] how i'm learning to soar...

Attitude is
a little
thing that
makes a big
difference.

[ ] Today's thoughts . . .

[ ] How I'm learning to soar . . .

Be anxious for nothing, but in everything by prayer and
supplication, with thanksgiving, let your requests be made
known to God; and the peace of God, which surpasses all
understanding, will guard your hearts and minds through
Christ Jesus.

PHILIPPIANS 4:6–7

[ ] Today's thoughts...

[ ] How I'm learning to soar...

You cannot
control
circumstances,
but you can
control your
response.

DATE
....

[ ] **Today's thoughts...**

[ ] **How I'm learning to soar...**

There is no fear in love;

but perfect love casts

out fear, because fear

involves torment. But he

who fears has not been

made perfect in love.

1 JOHN 4:18

[ ] Today's thoughts...

[ ] How I'm learning to soar...

Allow God's love to pierce through your pain.

[ ] today's thoughts...

[ ] how i'm learning to soar...

"He will yet fill your

mouth with laughing,

and your lips

with rejoicing."

JOB 8:21

[ ] today's thoughts...

[ ] how i'm learning to soar...

It's okay to hurt, but you have to heal.

DATE

....

[ ] Today's thoughts...

[ ] How I'm Learning to soar...

"For if you forgive

men their

trespasses, your

heavenly Father will

also forgive you.

But if you do not

forgive men their

trespasses, neither

will your Father

forgive your

trespasses."

MATTHEW 6:14–15

[ ] Today's thoughts...

[ ] How I'm learning to soar...

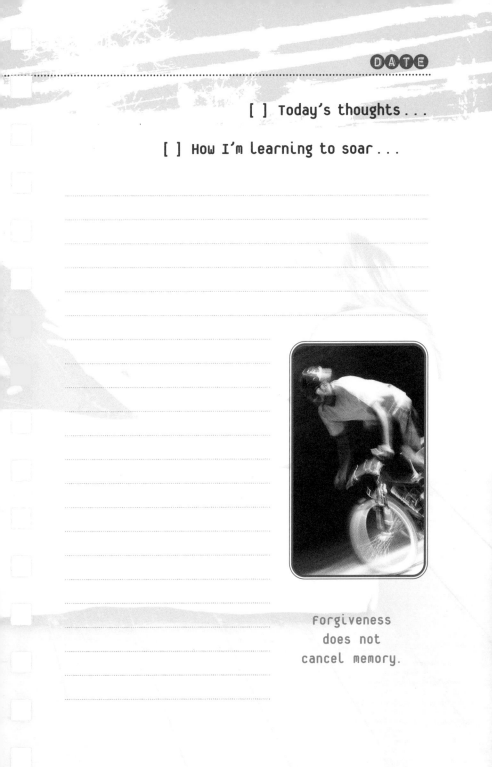

forgiveness
does not
cancel memory.

DATE

[ ] Today's thoughts...

[ ] How I'm learning to soar...

The LORD is my

shepherd; I shall

not want.

PSALM 23:1

[ ] Today's thoughts...

[ ] How I'm learning to soar...

When you can't
trace God's hand,
you can always
trust His heart.

DATE

[ ] *Today's thoughts...*

[ ] *How I'm learning to soar...*

She said to herself, "If only I may touch His garment, I shall be made well." But Jesus turned around, and when He saw her He said, "Be of good cheer, daughter; your faith has made you well." And the woman was made well from that hour.

MATTHEW 9:21–22

[ ] Today's thoughts...

[ ] How I'm learning to soar...

Expectancy
is the breeding
ground for
miracles.

[ ] Today's thoughts . . .

        [ ] How I'm learning to soar . . .

"This Book of the Law shall not depart from your mouth,
but you shall meditate in it day and night, that you may
observe to do according to all that is written in it. For then
you will make your way prosperous, and then you will
have good success."

JOSHUA 1:8

[ ] Today's thoughts...

[ ] How I'm learning to soar...

"Success" only
comes before
"work" in the
dictionary.

[ ] Today's thoughts...

[ ] How I'm learning to soar...

"Yet they seek Me daily, and delight to know My ways, as a nation that did righteousness, and did not forsake the ordinance of their God. They ask of Me the ordinances of justice; they take delight in approaching God."

ISAIAH 58:2

[ ] Today's thoughts . . .

[ ] How I'm learning to soar . . .

Successful people do daily what others do occasionally.

But Jesus looked at them and said, "With men it is impossible, but not with God; for with God all things are possible."

MARK 10:27

[ ] Today's thoughts...

[ ] How I'm learning to soar...

[ ] Today's thoughts...

[ ] How I'm learning to soar...

faith is what moves God.

As a teenager, Daniel was taken as a captive to the capital city of Israel's enemy, where he defied all the odds and rose to become the ruler over the whole province of Babylon (Daniel 2:48). Read his entire story and you'll discovered that Daniel's daring flight to become a world influencer came through the decisions he made to follow his God rather than compromise his values through peer pressure.

Take time to review the last several pages of this journal. Reflect on all the things you have been discovering about your life. As you've thought about your life in the light of God's Word, what are you learning? How is God teaching you to fly? What lessons and truths is He working in your life?

Capture your thoughts below.

REFLECTIONS

REFLECTIONS

Until you accept that God created you perfectly as you are,
you will try to be someone else, and that would be an imitation.